Poems, Tributes, and Dreams

BY GARY NADELEN

DORRANCE PUBLISHING CO
EST. 1920
PITTSBURGH, PENNSYLVANIA 15238

Dorrance Publishing Co
585 Alpha Drive
Suite 103
Pittsburgh, PA 15238
Visit our website at *www.dorrancebookstore.com*

ISBN: 979-8-88812-365-2
eISBN: 979-8-88812-865-7

Poems, Tributes, and Dreams

Introduction

Hopefully my poems and stories can give you peace
For a brief time maybe you can escape the world
Reading words from a stranger to make sorrow cease
My poems and stories take you to a world not found
Most all these writings come from dreams and vision
If I can take you to a new place you've never been
It makes my life worth it to help with your decision
If your life is heading you toward pain and sorrow
For a few minutes or more you go to a spot far away
Today was yesterday, now it's today until tomorrow
Fantasies become reality when tomorrow is today
This introduction started as a line, now is six stanzas
So if you always hated poetry, I hope that you enjoy?
So come with me on a trip from reality to what was
This trip will take you from the birth of our Nation
you'll meet a broken-hearted clown on a public bus
you'll meet my friends handy capped and aged
life can take many twists and turns we joke and kid
So as I share my life with you please enjoy this page

Peace and happiness

Your tour guide, the brokenhearted clown

Circles and squares

Laying on the deck looking up at the sky
Looking at the clouds and the shapes as they move
Drawing with my finger shapes as they move away
You watch the clouds form memories of lost love
You think back to when you were young and carefree
dreams of things you did when you had no worries
A bird flies by and you watch as he flies to a tree
Some more birds appear to your left in a flurry
For at least a while the sky and birds take you away
you escape to were ever your dreams take you
You take your finger and trace the clouds passing by
Each cloud has its shapes, forms as it goes through
With your finger trace the clouds circles and squares
As you dream and you trace clouds it brings fears
You think of friends gone now life isn't fair
You continue to trace shapes circles and squares
The shapes in the sky begin to move blown by wind
Circles and squares become trains, planes, and cars
You get a phone call from miles away, an old friend
Now your thoughts go to clouds circles and squares
Your old friend remembers dreams of the clouds
We share our dreams tracing circles and squares

Hind Sight Is 20/20

Today I was exchanging emails with my old friend
She sent me the writings from a gifted writer
Our mails started with conversations from back then
She began with her stressful job she'd been given
She was afraid the skills needed were beyond her
Being the wise mentor she thinks, she asked advice
Sometimes friends try hard to be more than they are
I sometimes feel what I suggest falls on deaf ears
I wrote a rather long note using my life experiences
My note was exposing my weakness and my fears
Not knowing she was unable to respond to my help
A short response, I felt hurt she had missed my point
I laid out my pains, was she missing what I felt?
We have no right to communicate, could cause rage
She has a wonderful man who loves her to a fault
Late in the day she wrote beautifully from the heart
She obviously read every word I felt like a jerk
Her answer made me feel stupid for doubting her
She explained she got caught up in very hard work
I now realize how vulnerable I am, she took my fear
I should have known she had no time to write then.
In our chats we refer to each other as dear friend
Her inspirational writer has many words of wisdom
Hind site, like water under the bridge, is 20/20
Sorry my friend for doubting you

One Strange Cat

You've probably heard of "the cat in the hat"
Doctor Seuss obviously didn't know my cat Dora
My cat has her own story to tell funnier than that
When my kitten came home I had no name for her
It so happens my granddaughter was visiting me
Her favorite character of course Dora the explorer
As the cat was into everything nothings safe you see
I had a stuffed owl that Dora would carry by the tail
She'd come with that owl much larger the cat was
But all this has nothing to do with "cat in the hat"
or why my cat is so strange this is because
She'll come from were she is when I run the faucet
I don't know what she gets from the drops that fall
It can't be because she's thirsty or dehydrated yet
She will sit in the sink for hours at a time that's all
She'll be sleeping in another room when I run it
I hear the patter of little feet then she's in the sink
She waits for the last drop to fall so she gets a sip
So that's why I call her the cat in the sink, just think
That's the story of the cat in the sink
      Story of my strange cat

Why I'm Proud To Be An American

Have you ever wondered why we solute the flag
Put a hand over our heart when fallen are laid to rest
By taking a knee at sporting events only shows hate
They show disrespect for the best of the best
Show their ignorance of what our flag is about
They show us they don't belong here show the door
They gave life or limb, gives them the right to shout
Love of country for us is what the flag stands for
This is to tell the history of those who fought for us
Let's take the time to tell about our nations birth
Back to 56 men who penned a petition to England
They tell George the 3rd in 1775, End England's curse
13 colonies of the continental congress vote separate
the 56 men send the Declaration of Independence
The Colonial Army of farmers, arm for their fate
They fought taxes, tyranny to give freedom a chance
Francis Scott Key wrote his famous poem
at Fort Mchenry the rockets and bombs burst in air
At daybreak Key saw our flag was still flying strong
words key wrote that night now show why we care
This is the birth of our nation for which we pray
now the flag flies over buildings, forts ships at sea
When you stand for honor and the American way
tum your back to the cowards who still take a knee
We have many reasons to respect our flag of our past
Battles at Lexington and concord prove we can fight
"Don't shoot until you see the whites of their eyes"
Battle cry for Bunker Hill, fought for what's right

"A day that will live in infamy" Pearl Harbors cry
Admiral Yamamoto "we awakened a sleeping giant"
Marines raised the flag at Mt Suribachi for victory
The Japanese found the United States can be defiant
Battles at Guam, Okinawa, Coral sea, Tarawa Atol
Our brave dive bombers at the battle of Midway
We lost over 90% of our planes but still met the call
they sunk or disabled two of three aircraft carriers that day
On the eastern front paratroopers land at huge loss
B 17 flying fortresses fly daytime raids on the rails
costing many to the Luftwalfs and flack were lost
our finest bombers with 11 men fall in death spirals
D day landings on 6/6/1944 against fortified beaches
machine gun fire hitting the ramp was curtain death
They knew very few would make shore out of reach
3,000 men would be shot or drown in the deep water
America's finest died to end the war to end all wars
Back to the pacific B 25 bombers on the Hornet
Under General Doolittle they do the impossible
Launch to bomb Tokyo to repay for Pearls vet
General MacArthur promise's the Philippine's
His famous promise "I shall return" to his regret
Victory in the Pacific signed on the Missouri
VJ day, Sept. 2, 1945 ends the war in the Pacific
General Eisenhower shows Germany our fury
Axis powers surrender on VE day ends conflict
At Reim's France on May 8,1945 they surrender
Troops come home to parades to show our pride
But all who say wars have ended are a pretender
The world has been at war we call them conflict
  our conflict in Korea, bloody war north V south

troops led by MacArthur get to China's boarder
From 1950 to July 1953 for the 38th parallel
The first war we've lost has a demilitarized area
No man's zone between north and south we fell
We entered Vietnam to help the French dilemma
From 11, 1955 until 4, 1975 soldiers fight in hell
Jungle war fare, agent orange, helicopter lz area
The evacuation of Saigon will end America's part
Our cost was 57,000 soldiers, now defoliant fear
our country now fights Afghanistan for their part
when 9/11/2001 Bin Laden attacks our homeland
for 20 years later we end America's longest war
Then we attack Iraq and Hussein's and's in sand
Our men and women go there to get even over there
We planted our flag in their sand we made our stand
That's why our flag flies for our greatest generation
We honor our flag battered torn but never beaten
We are still free and we are still the greatest nation
So remember our fallen heroes, our women and men
I'm not a hero but I served and walked with some
When you hear our national anthem stand tall
Show respect for our greatest say thanks for freedom
Thank God to live in the home of the brave and free
I've tried to write this like a poem it's hard to rhyme
To honor those who lost limb and life to be free
      Thank God whenever you can
To live in the home of the brave and land of the free
      This is why
I stand for the National Anthem and the fallen
Why I'm proud to be an American

"I'm No Hero"

Every day they rush into burning buildings
Or face a bad guy armed and wishing them harm
Or on a battlefield they lay down there life
        For home and country
they're just doing the job that they love.
I'm no hero, but I've had the honor to walk with the
hero's who've served doing what they do everyday
I'm no hero, but I walk among heroes daily

        For those who died on 9/11/2001
        Just doing their job

Looking For Peace

After high school, I had no plans
Fate would change all that, as I would soon find out
I thought I knew—the man I wanted to be
And I would find my way, as far as I could be
 I went to college to better my life
But college wasn't for me or what I wanted to be
Little did I know my path was chosen for me
My draft notice came to direct my course
 I thought I would be married with a family
 But for me now it was not to be
I joined the Navy to see the world
 Looking for peace
In the Navy, I learned to be a good leader
I figured my life was the sea, that wouldn't be my life
after the Navy, I found a great job
 I got married and gave it a try, our family included
sons having a wife would soon end married life would cease
 Life would go through changes
 While looking for peace
ladies would come and ladies would go
Bar hoping and partying, while looking for love
Life with the ladies would come to an end
Leaving many ladies behind, I loved them all
I would meet the one lady I regret leaving behind
 Still looking for peace
She now has her man, he's her best friend
 She's his wife
 I wish them the very best of life

I hope they have many happy trails
So my future is now in God's hands
I wait for his plan
Still looking for peace

Jesus Walking On Water

My sons and I were camping at a local beach. We decided to take my 14' open boat with its 35 hp outboard motor, I'll call it the minnow, so we packed up to go on a three-hour cruise. We were going fishing; our goal was to go about eight miles to the Ducks Island group. The Ducks are well into the open water of Lake Ontario. After about three or so hours, we arrived. The Ducks are a very popular place to fish. We no sooner wet a line when a huge storm hit with very heavy rain, high winds and about five foot waves. Now to set up the situation, my boat has no floatation, and with the 35 hp motor, it might reach a speed of 30 mph. We packed up our gear and started towards the mainland. As I said before, about eight miles.

The wind was picking up and the waves were off-shore, meaning we would have to climb each wave like a steep hill. I was afraid the boat wasn't up to the trip; truth is, the boat wasn't up to the task at ahead of us. I told the boys to put on their life jackets and look for something to bail out the boat. This had turned from a nice day of fishing into a life-or-death situation, that little 35 hp motor had to push up the waves then down the other side where the waves would wash over the bow, putting more water into the boat. I'm not ashamed to say I was very afraid we would not make it to shore. If, for whatever the reason, we would get sideways we would capsize and they wouldn't find us till we washed up on shore. With every wave we went over made me think of the little train that said, "I think I can."

Thinking back, there's no way that little boat should make shore. "If not for the courage of the fearless crew, the minnow would be lost." After what seemed like many hours of that little motor getting us back.

Finally, we could see the shoreline and we knew we had made it. It was like a heavy load had subsided and my thoughts were drained.

Looking back, I know I was so focused on getting us back, I didn't take time to pray or give thanks to God. Thinking of Matthew 14, thinking of Jesus walking on water,

I can see that Jesus was walking on the water.

Next to us.

When The Eagle Takes Flight

Have you ever wondered why during the night
The owl searches in the darkness for his prey
Why the wolf comes out to howl at moonlight
The fox leaves his lair to go out to play
WHEN THE EAGLE TAKES FLIGHT
The bear leaves his cave looking for some berries and nuts
The blue jay becomes the warning crier of the woods
The male deer rubs his antlers before he goes into rut
Bugs come out at night as the lowest in the chain of food
WHEN THE EAGLE TAKES FLIGHT
The raccoon searches anywhere to eat at night
The squirrel gathers nuts and seeds for winter
The wolverine, the tough guy looking for a fight
The opossum comes out from his daytime slumber
WHEN THE EAGLE TAKES FLIGHT
The prairie dog climbs out from his hole
The bull frog sings his mournful crocking song
You see the ground move from the digging mole
All life great or small live all the day long
WHEN THE EAGLE TAKES FLIGHT
Now take the animals out of this equation
Now place people who fight for what is right
Place yourself in trying to protect our nation
Look to the sky and see the EAGLE TAKES TO FLIGHT.
PEACE THROUGH STRENGTH

The Broken-Hearted Clown

This story is about the clowns that cry
As they play the fool or jester to make you smile
They're all around you telling jokes you wonder why
They hide their tears and all fears for a while

You'll find them on street comers and alleyways
Trying to make you laugh to hide their fears
They joke about themselves to make us forget today
Though you don't know it he's laughing to hide tears
Making people laugh is how he puts the day away

History tells the story of the court jester's tale
The fool with pointed hat and curled toe shoes
What he hides with jokes really hides that he's frail
While he leaves the crowd laughing, he's in the blues

Clowns like EMMITT KELLY, the best of them all
His face was always made up with a frown
His famous character "Weary Willie" was his call
He's known as the first and best of all clown's.

The clown is not always excepted as himself
The sad clown comes on like he's loved by all
Try though he does, the clown goes on the shelf
He then becomes himself waiting for his final call

I'm no comedian, but I play one on the bus
Making fun of myself and friend's one and all

They seem to have fun and rarely make a fuss
When I leave the bus oh to be a fly on the wall

I'd know if my humor is funny to others
Do I leave them laughing with me this I hope
Sometimes I feel I've gone too far am I a bother
To get along with all others and not just a dope

I ride the bus nearly ever day to cure a frown
I would love to know that no one is offended
If only one person changes to a smile from a frown
I've done my job as God intended
       For I am The Broken Hearted Clown

A Long Way To Heaven

FROM A DREAM BY GARY NADELEN

All the day through we long for the Lord
Seeking out in all the usual hiding places
But all day long we listen for his word
If it makes you cry to think you can't find a trace
      A LONG WAY TO HEAVEN
You're told time and time again wait on God
You listen for God's or an angle's voice
You seek God's friendship when you deserve the rod
You're seeking seems useless but you have no choice
      A LONG WAY TO HEAVEN
If it was easy then everyone would be there
So being only human you follow the wide road
Peace doesn't come to you so you ask "does he care"
So you go your own way, but find he's not there
      A LONG WAY TO HEAEN
You know that God say's for man it's impossible
But at the end of the day our tears are times seven
You've stumbled and fallen to still make you able
Salvation is from God but it's a long way to Heaven

I Wonder Why

All my life I've wondered why
God does the things he does
I wonder why birds can fly
And babies have to learn to crawl
before they learn to walk
     I WONDER WHY
Life comes and for all life goes
And one day we all will die
Why we have ten fingers and ten toes
If I had a clue it would be a lie
     I WONDER WHY
When we are young, strong, and brave
We spend our youth searching for fun
Life is very short and time we cannot save
Only God knows when our days are done
     I WONDER WHY
We try to love friends and foe
Knowing we should keep our friends close
And why we keep our enemies at the door
We live our lives trying to get the most
     I WONDER WHY
Why God keeps our lives a secret
And we don't know when we will die
If we've been good enough to have no regret
Why God loves us enough to wonder why
     I WONDER WHY
Only God knows how long our lives will go
How long we'll wonder through this place

God will decide if we are goats or sheep
the end will come we know not why
      I WONDER WHY
At the end times both God and angels cry
Because so many of us will go to hell
We'll not know until we give it a try
For now we have to say why God won't tell
      I WONDER WHY

Let Our Light Shine

INSPIRED BY THE SONG BY RAY REPP
"I AM THE LIGHT"

Once again it's after midnight and I'm inspired to write
I just finished watching the mass on EWTN
The theme of the mass was "let our light shine"
This reminded me of a Christian folk singer
His name is Ray Repp, he used to come to our youth
Ralleys, he could fire up the crowd with his songs
He had many tapes, I have one here somewhere
Unfortunately they are on cassette tapes
So I can only play them on my portable player, I do
However I have his music saved on my phone.
The name of the song is "I am the light" it was during
One of his concerts that the whole auditorium shock.
I asked others if they felt it, everyone had felt it.
After the mass they gave a quote from St Augustine of
Hippo, when he talked of the disciples after the sermon on
the mount, Jesus stayed behind to pray, while the disciples
got into their boat and went on ahead. A huge storm came
up, they were afraid when they saw Jesus walking
ahead on the water, they thought he was a ghost, Jesus
walked on ahead and waited for them on the shore. When
he walked by them the storm calmed, when he arrived he
explained to them that, when asked about it, he said.
"I am the light of the world." I was inspired to listen to
Ray Repp "I am the light."

My Cat's Favorite Toy

My cat's all time favorite toy
If you really want to call it that
His favorite thing that gives him joy
His favorite toy is a winter hat

This hat he'll play with and even wrestle
Sometimes there worn to cover your ears
My hat is black and red striped with a tassel
It's like Linus's blanket to hide his fears

Some cats have a stuffed bird or a mouse
 My cat wants nothing to do with that
It doesn't matter if you fill a toy with catnip
He'll search all over the house for that hat

If you hide it or try to take it away
Instead of to eat, drink, or sleep
He'll come dragging that hat every day
Throughout the day until he finds it, not a peep

Late at night when you lay down your head
You'll hear his mournful cry while you try to sleep
He'll drag none other than that old hat to bed
Then he'll curl up with it at your feet

Water Under The Bridge

In the past, my writings I've said yesterday is gone
Yesterday is behind us, we can't return, if you plan
You plan making our nation like before strong
To make us a better place, past be gone make a stand
Don't keep looking back at where we were then
We fought a war for independence to beat tyranny
Our flag flies everywhere freedom makes its stand
We need to move on don't let cowards take a knee
We must fight like we did in 1776 leave our brand
Let's get back to when we were brave and free
and show we're still willing and able to take a stand
Then we can show the world we're all we can be
Be willing to stand up for our fallen who defend us
stay free and thank our uniformed women and men
be aware of older General's with the liberal agenda
be careful know that some officer's aren't friends
when a coward takes a knee show him the door
Fear not after all you already know he's a coward
Remember the flag is for brave who have seen war
Water under the bridge like yesterday's gone forever
The woke coward can never change his stripes ever

The Water Returned Under The Bridge

Yesterday I was chatting with my best friend
And it inspired me to write the following poem
We talked about many things and old trends
She gave me a song to listen to, "Broken Arrow"
She told me water in a bottle made her remember
I told her to listen to "I'm never gonna dance again"
"Broken Arrow" is a beautiful song about her. We
chatted back and forth about things from back then
Time and time again I've said yesterday's gone away
And water under the bridge can't return were it was
These songs made us remember about time gone by
It's 2:30 a.m. now but I must finish writing because
Playing those songs from then made me wonder
Whether all these years I've said you can't go back
yesterday is now today and gone forever I wonder
Yesterday the water under the bridge has gone back
For one day yesterday came back for us both
The water under the bridge from where it came
from miles and years apart, we went back
The water returned under the bridge for us one time

Is My Dad Still Here

For Dad

By His Son Gary

Many times I've sat here in my mom's chair
Across from where my dad was when he left us
I wasn't there that day, I was in my car heading there
returning home after shooting clay target at sackets
My sister Margaret, crying, called my car phone
The words she spoke brought a tear to my eye
I could hear her sob as she told me, "Daddy's gone"
To this day I regret I was not able to say goodbye
When I got there the family were all gathered there
No one that was there were ashamed to cry
The funeral home people loaded Dad with care
Scott didn't come in to see Grandpa that way
They took Dad away on the stretcher to the hearse
That brings me to where Dad laid in that big room
Now I sit in Mom's chair looking were he passed
There's a presence here that I can only assume
Are the things that happens day or mostly night
Dad is gone from here physically gone too soon
While watching television I sometimes see a light
This light appears and darts across the dining room
during the day the movement is more subtle
During the day I see movement should I fear
The possibility haunts me is it possible
IS MY DAD STILL HERE

Late Life Crisis

Morning arrives in its usual way without warning
Another day brings a new day of day dreams
So you get up, have breakfast as always, boring
You know your new day is never what it seems
You know you have many choices to make
The new day holds many new surprises
So you stare out the window until you awake
That's how you begin your day in a late life crisis
Now you proceed to catch the public transportation
On the bus you have friends, all shapes and sizes
For an hour and a half you have many conversations
No real destination you continue your late life crisis
Some with walkers, wheelchairs, crutches, and canes
Like you they spend their lives, for the golden years
Be careful what you wish for in all lives there is rain
After shopping you return to the late life crisis
There are no GOLDEN YEARS, just late life crisis

"Full Circle"

(FOR THE WOKE GENERATION)

Well, here they are, finally out of school
　　　Now looking for a job
They've tried college or working with tools
Some go work with the office crowd

All of their lives they've waited for this day
　　　When they'll work to pay their bills
Followed the crowd to see what they would say
Everything they've tried to do just gives us chills

So now it's time to call it quits and cry uncle
They look to the state to give them their money
I guess it looks like they've gone full circle
They end up back home with Daddy and Mommy
　　　From a dream 9/15/2022

When you wake up from a dream
Did the dream come from seeking God
It's a split second before you wake that you recall
If you dream about the past you lived
As the day goes by that it's when you give your all
Maybe it's about what today you have to give
remember that when you dream of yesterday
Yesterday is gone forever, now you have today
after today all you have is the future
If you've lived your life for doing good maybe
God will say you've become mature
So join me good and loyal servant as you would
Take up my cross and follow me
Because maybe tomorrow will never come
So by following me you will have all you need be
Live your life to be all you can be
Maybe if you've helped just one person today
Maybe then your life will be worthy
Maybe you'll pay down your sins and you can say
This will help to make your soul healthy
If you've tried to be a good servant
When Jesus says, "do this in memory of me."
And you will look to God and say (here I am Lord).

Peace On Earth

My first story is a fantasy based on characters from *The Peanuts* cartoons by Charles Schulz of Snoopy the America ace beagle flyer and the Bloody Red Baron, German ace, and Snoopy's pursuit of the Baron over the skies of Germany, put to the famous words in song by the Royal Guardsmen.

Snoopy finds the Red Baron and begins his attack
It wasn't long before a dog fight of the two aces
The baron was a far more experienced a fact
Wasn't long before Snoopy realized what he faces
The Baron forced Snoopy down behind enemy lines
The Baron swung around for the finishing kill
He turned on our hero and flew by several times
He made one more pass to make this pass the end
The Baron waved Merry Christmas my friend
To this day our hero Snoopy will never know
Was it the songs coming from the missions below

The next story is a true story of a Christmas miracle.
This story begins in WWI, on the eastern front.

STORY #2

We begin this story in the trenches on the east front
The date is December 24, 1914 trench to trench
Allied soldiers cold and wet fight across for ground

Man to man fighting for yards of land at a time
On the eve of Christmas alleys hear songs abound
From the German trenches came songs of the time
Silent night came from across the no man's ground
The Allies joined in from there trenches in rhyme
from the German side came a soldier with white flag
The allies sent a white flag to meet the enemy sign
Before long the trenches emptied together no rage
After exchanging handshakes talked about the time
The allies had a soccer ball and a game ensued
Each side said they won, 3/2 Allies, 4/3 Germans
But by now no one really cared after saying adieu
Christmas day they sang songs and as if friends
That night they said there goodbyes combat resumes
For one Christmas they will not forget now ends
The cease fire ends the truce of 12/25/14 war ensues
The whole event was recorded in the London news.

STORY #3

The third miracle is December 24, 1944, WW2

This is a lesser known story
As told by Fritz Vincken, he was a 12-year-old boy
Fritz tells the story to the Readers Digest Jan. 1973 Fritz and
his mother had moved into a cabin from their home that was de-
stroyed by an advancing American offensive in their village.

The story begins with 12-year-old Fritz with mother
Into a cabin in the Huertgen forest near the warfare

at the battle of the Bulge's heavy, fighting their
They answered a knock at the door, three soldiers
standing there they were Americans wet and cold
mother Vincken invited them in one was wounded
she didn't speak English letting them in was bold
aiding the enemy was treason but let them and found
in broken French they put Harry the wounded one
In her own bed she treated his injuries his friends
were Jim and Robin they told her they were lost
they had wandered three days looking for their lines
she prepared a meal of potatoes and rooster roast
while it was cooking there came a knock at the door
Fritz answered there stood four German soldiers
The German soldiers were searching for their troops
mother expected more Americans now was in fear
the German corporal asked if they could rest there
mother explained about the American's resting here
she said let's stop the killing at least for Christmas
the Germans put their weapons at the door there
Americans put their weapons were the door was
the mixed group all sat down and shared the meal
two Germans were 16 the corporal 23 was oldest
mother said grace Komm herr, Jesus, made it real
they all had tears as the looked out at the bright star
in the sky outside that holiest of nights made it feel
that the moments of the truce must end back to war.
They parted as friends then back to what was real
The war took a time out it seemed like war is afar
This became none as the "truce in the forest"
   Thank you to Fritz a 12-year-old boy
for a short time there was peace for nine strange friends

www.ingramcontent.com/pod-product-compliance
Lightning Source LLC
Chambersburg PA
CBHW061647130726
47996CB00003B/1502